Recording Podcasts

By Kristin Fontichiaro

Published in the United States of America by:

CHERRY LAKE PRESS

2395 South Huron Parkway, Suite 200, Ann Arbor, Michigan
www.cherrylakepublishing.com

Series Adviser: Kristin Fontichiaro
Reading Adviser: Marla Conn, MS, Ed., Literacy specialist, Read-Ability, Inc.
Book Designer: Felicia Macheske
Character Illustrator: Rachael McLean

Photo Credits: © Branislav Nenin/Shutterstock.com, 7; © wavebreakmedia/Shutterstock.com, 15; © paffy/Shutterstock.com, 19

Graphics Throughout: © the simple surface/Shutterstock.com; © Diana Rich/Shutterstock.com; © lemony/Shutterstock.com;
© CojoMoxon/Shutterstock.com; © IreneArt/Shutterstock.com; © Artefficient/Shutterstock.com; © Marie Nimrichterova/Shutterstock.
com; © Svetolk/Shutterstock.com; © EV-DA/Shutterstock.com; © briddy/Shutterstock.com; © Mix3r/Shutterstock.com

Library of Congress Cataloging-in-Publication Data

Names: Fontichiaro, Kristin, author. | McLean, Rachael, illustrator.
Title: Recording podcasts / by Kristin Fontichiaro ; illustrated by Rachael McLean.
Description: Ann Arbor, Michigan : Cherry Lake Publishing, 2020. | Series:
 Create and share : thinking digitally | Includes index. | Audience:
 Grades 2-3.
Identifiers: LCCN 2019033414 (print) | LCCN 2019033415 (ebook) | ISBN
 9781534159136 (hardcover) | ISBN 9781534161436 (paperback) | ISBN
 9781534160286 (pdf) | ISBN 9781534162587 (ebook)
Subjects: LCSH: Podcasting—Juvenile literature.
Classification: LCC TK5105.887 .F66 2020 (print) | LCC TK5105.887 (ebook)
 | DDC 302.23/4—dc23
LC record available at https://lccn.loc.gov/2019033414
LC ebook record available at https://lccn.loc.gov/2019033415

Cherry Lake Publishing would like to acknowledge the work of the Partnership for 21st Century Learning, a Network of Battelle
for Kids. Please visit www.battelleforkids.org/networks/p21 for more information.

Printed in the United States of America
Corporate Graphics

Table of CONTENTS

CHAPTER ONE

What's a Podcast?

Do you like acting out plays or skits? Asking people questions? Recording your voice with friends on a phone or **device**? If you said yes to any of these questions, you might like podcasting!

A podcast is an **audio** recording that is shared online. You can record your voice or musical instruments. You can even add music or sound effects. These added effects make your podcast come alive. When you finish recording, you can share it online. You might save it in an **app** like Seesaw. You can also use Apple Podcasts or Google Play to share your podcast with the world. But you will need an adult's permission and help with services like those.

Research

Let's get to know some podcasts for kids! You can find these through your device's podcast store or by searching for them online. Remember, always ask a trusted adult for help and permission.

A FEW OF OUR FAVORITE PODCASTS:

Storytelling
Circle Round from WBUR
Storynory

Science
But Why: A Podcast for Curious Kids from Vermont Public Radio

Ideas
Brains On! from Minnesota Public Radio

As you listen, think about these questions:

- How long is it?
- What is it about?
- What is the style?
    - Serious
    - Funny
- How is the podcast organized?
    - What happens at the beginning and the end?
- How do music and sound effects make the show more interesting?

People make podcasts about the things they care about. They might talk about little-known facts. Some people review sports games. Some podcasts are interviews with people. Your friend who plays guitar may want to record her guitar solos. Your theater friends may want to act out their favorite stories by using **dialogue**. If you can record it and share it online, it's a podcast!

To start a podcast, you will need:

- Device: a computer, tablet, or smartphone
- Internet connection
- Podcasting software or an app that records audio, like GarageBand, Audacity, Voice Memo, Seesaw, or Anchor
- **Microphone** (or one built into your device)
- Website where you can post your podcast
- An adult's permission

Your librarian or teacher may have supplies you can use.

CHAPTER TWO

Planning

Skilled podcasters make a plan before they start recording. This helps them feel calmer when the microphone is turned on. Let's practice planning by thinking about a commercial. Commercials, or ads, are designed to grab the listener's attention and encourage them to buy or do something. A short ad is a great first recording!

Think about what you want to sell. Ads can sell a product, like toys or cars. They can sell a service, like lawn mowing or babysitting. Some ads sell experiences, like vacations or upcoming concerts. Ads can also **persuade** people to do something, like protect the planet or stay healthy. Those ads are called public service announcements, or PSAs.

Ads and podcasts share these four elements:

HOOK
Grabs the listener's attention in an exciting way. This could be exciting words, music, or a sound effect.

INFORMATION
Tells the listener why your product is great. This gives them more information about your service.

ACTION
Tells people what you want them do to.

MEMORABLE ENDING
Wraps up your ad in an interesting way.

Your Turn!

Let's record a quick podcast. First, we need to plan it out.

INSTRUCTIONS:

1. Pick a topic. What do you want to talk about?
   - Favorite book ✓
   - Movie you're excited to watch
   - Sporting event
2. Think about the purpose of your podcast. Try to be specific.
   - Do you want to help advertise the book? ✓
   - Do you want to talk about that exciting ending? (If so, be sure to warn your listeners. They might not have read the book!)
3. Once you have your topic and purpose narrowed down, start writing your **script**!

   HINT: Start with your **hook**. Then add the **information**, **action**, and a **memorable ending**.
4. Share your script with a trusted friend or family member. Ask for their thoughts and a helpful **critique**.
5. Revise your script based on the feedback you get.
6. Practice saying it over and over, until you feel relaxed as you talk.

What if a chocolate bar could change your life forever? Charlie buys a chocolate bar and finds a Golden Ticket inside. Now he and Grandpa Joe are off to Willy Wonka's chocolate factory. Inside are amazing smells and colors— even a chocolate river! Charlie meets other kids with a Golden Ticket. Boy, are they awful! And awful things keep happening to them. What lies ahead for Charlie inside the factory? Find out when you read *Charlie and the Chocolate Factory* by Roald Dahl. You'll never look at chocolate the same way again.

CHAPTER THREE

Recording

You're almost ready to record now! It's time to talk with an adult about which recording app is best for you. Your teacher might want to protect your **privacy**. She might encourage you to pick an app like Seesaw. This app allows only classmates and family to listen to your recording.

Does your family want to start a podcast? Do they want to publish it so that anyone in the world can stream it? If so, you might want to use an app like Anchor. Once you have your app picked out, practice with it a little bit. Then record!

Time to Record

You're finally ready to record!

INSTRUCTIONS:

1. Gather the equipment listed in chapter 1.
2. Set up your equipment in a quiet place.
3. Have your script readily available.
4. Review your software's buttons or **icons** so you know how to start and stop recording.
5. When you are ready to record:
   - Take a deep breath.
   - Press the record button.
   - Speak slowly and clearly.
   - Press Stop when you are done.

You did it! Play back your recording. Your voice might sound different, but that's normal. Pay attention to the recording. Can you clearly hear what's being said? If you like what you recorded, save it. If not, delete it and record it again.

CHAPTER FOUR

Adding Music or Sound Effects

A podcast with your voice is great. Adding music or sound effects can make it even better. Music sets the mood of a recording. It can make your recording happy, sad, or scary. Sound effects help listeners imagine things they can't see. For example, your friend may want his listeners to think he is in a spaceship. He might add weird space sounds like whooshes. He may want to add sounds like people clicking buttons to run the spaceship.

With simple software like Voice Memo, you will want to gather up objects and make sound effects right as you record. Take your shoes off and "walk" them on the table if you need footsteps. Borrow musical instruments from your music teacher. Pour water from a pitcher into a tub if you need interesting underwater sounds. Get creative!

What sounds will you record?

Other software lets you edit by adding **tracks**. You can record sound effects separately and add them later or find them online. Some software comes with built-in music and effects.

You need permission to use other people's recordings, unless they have given it a Creative Commons license. This tells others it is okay to use their recording. It's also a lot of fun to make your own!

You can make your own sound effects library. This is what Foley artists do for a living. They are always listening for new and interesting sounds they find in their world. They record ordinary things like vacuum cleaners and then manipulate the sound.

Take your recording device around your school and think about what sounds you could record. How about a door slamming? The recess bell? How would you use the sound of a squeaky marker on a whiteboard? Want to record people chatting at school or in the cafeteria? If so, don't forget to ask the people you're recording for permission before hitting that "record" button!

CHAPTER FIVE

Editing, Exporting, Sharing

It is important to review your recording. Make sure it sounds just right. Sometimes, it takes a couple of tries. You might find things you want to change or fix. Some podcast recording apps let you remove sections that you don't like. They might let you make some parts louder or rearrange sections. This is called editing.

Combine your music, voice, and sound effects. Edit the recording until it sounds like something you'd hear on the radio or a podcast. Then talk to an adult about how to post it so others can listen. After you've uploaded your recording, you can start planning your next **episode**!

Will your podcast be a stand-alone episode or part of a series?

Time to Edit

Editing is an important part of recording a podcast. The process helps your recording sound great. Here are a few questions to think about when editing:

Am I too quiet?

If so, move your mouth closer to the microphone. Some podcast recording apps and software have special editing tools to boost the volume.

Do I have dead air?

Radio announcers call moments of unwanted silence "dead air." There could be dead air at the beginning or end of your recording. Dead air might also happen when you pause. It can happen when someone you are interviewing doesn't answer right away. Cut those empty spots. You'll sound more like a professional!

Do my words make sense?

It's always fine to record again if you get a new, better idea. Go back to the same place where you recorded the first time. That way, the background noise will sound the same.

After editing, you are ready to **export** and publish your recording. This turns it into an internet-friendly format. Follow your software or app's instructions.

Your podcast is now ready for an audience. Time to share it! You can email it to friends or family. You can also save it to your Seesaw account or Google Drive. Or post it to your class's website. If you want the world to hear it, ask a trusted adult for help and permission to publish it.

Congratulations, podcaster! You've learned a fun and creative way to share your thoughts and talents with others.

GLOSSARY

app (APP) a computer program, usually on a smartphone or tablet

audio (AW-dee-oh) having to do with how sound is heard, recorded, and played back

critique (krih-TEEK) a careful and helpful opinion someone gives about the good and bad parts of something

device (dih-VISE) a term used to describe a computing object such as a smartphone, laptop, or tablet

dialogue (DYE-uh-lawg) conversation

episode (EP-ih-sode) one program in a series

export (EK-sport) to create a copy of a computer file in a different format so it can be used with another program

Foley artists (FOH-lee AR-tists) people who make sound effects for a living, usually for movies

icons (EYE-kahnz) graphic symbols on the desktop of a computer screen representing programs, functions, or files

manipulate (muh-NIP-yuh-late) to handle or control something skillfully

microphone (MYE-kruh-fone) an instrument used to record sound or make sound louder

persuade (pur-SWADE) to convince someone to do or believe something by giving the person good reasons

privacy (PRYE-vuh-see) a state in which others do not disturb or interfere with your personal matters

script (SKRIPT) written text of a play, movie, television show, radio show, or commercial

tracks (TRAKS) "layers" of audio that you can edit separately or combine on top of one another in an audio editing program

For More INFORMATION

BOOKS

Higgins, Nadia. *Making a Podcast*. Mankato, Minnesota: Amicus, 2019.

Hudak, Heather C. *Creative Podcast Producer*s. Minneapolis, Minnesota: ABDO, 2019.

WEBSITES

Anchor
https://anchor.fm
This site will help you record, edit, and share your podcast with the world.

Creative Commons Search
https://oldsearch.creativecommons.org
People add a Creative Commons license to their work when they want other people to use it. It's giving permission in advance. Use this search engine to find great music and sound for your podcasts!

INDEX

About the AUTHOR

Kristin Fontichiaro teaches at the University of Michigan School of Information and writes books for adults and kids. She listens to a lot of podcasts. *Circle Round* is one of her favorites.